Jesus Is Born

Jesus Is Born

by Rolf Krenzer
with illustrations by Constanza Droop

Translation by
Linda M. Maloney

A Liturgical Press Book

THE LITURGICAL PRESS
Collegeville, Minnesota

Joseph, the carpenter from Nazareth, looked suspiciously at the woman he was about to marry. "An angel, you say?" he asked. "God sent an angel to you?" Mary nodded.

Mary had never lied to Joseph. And she had never seemed to him so serious as she was now. There was a light in her eyes that he had never seen before.

"I was so frightened when he stood before me," said Mary softly. "The angel said: 'Be happy, Mary! God has something great planned for you!'"

Mary, of all people: could God have great plans for *her*?

"I was afraid," Mary said. "But the angel said that I did not need to fear. And he said: 'Mary, you have found favor with God.'"

Joseph said nothing. He thought for a long time. "Then God has chosen you," he said at last. Mary nodded. "God has a special plan for me," she said. "I will bear a son. He is to be named Jesus, and he will be king of heaven and earth. God is his father. He is God's Son!"

Joseph was silent. He simply could not believe what Mary was telling him. "Did the angel tell you that?" he asked at last. Mary nodded. "And you?" Joseph asked. "What did you say?"

"I said, 'Let it be as you have said!'" Mary whispered.

Then Joseph knew that Mary was happy about the baby, the child that was God's own.

"I want to be for God, all the time and with my whole heart," said Mary.

And Joseph began to be happy, too.

Another messenger had come to Nazareth. This one was from the emperor. He read out the words telling what the powerful ruler in Rome had said: "The emperor wants to know how many people live in his empire. So all the people must go to the places their families came from and let themselves be enrolled. Then they can go home again."

More than two thousand years ago, the Romans had built a powerful world empire. It reached all the way to Israel. It was ruled by the Emperor Augustus in Rome, and King Herod in Jerusalem had to obey him.

So it was that Mary and Joseph had to make the trip, too. Joseph was born in a little town called Bethlehem. The way there was long and hard. They were poor people who could not buy or rent a wagon. Mary was pregnant, and her baby would be born very soon.

After many days, when they came to Bethlehem, they could not find a place to stay anywhere. In the end they had to stay in a stable with a manger. That was where they would spend the night.

During that night Mary bore a son. Her first baby! God's Son! She wrapped the baby in bands of cloth and laid it in the straw in the manger.

That night, some shepherds were tending their sheep on the fields near Bethlehem. In the middle of the night God sent an angel to them.

When the shepherds woke up, they were amazed to see God's bright light shining around them. They were filled with surprise and fear.

But the angel said to them: "Don't be afraid! I will tell you something that will bring joy to all people. Today is born to you in Bethlehem a Savior, Christ the Lord! He will be king of heaven and earth. He is God's Son, the one God promised to you and to all people."

Then the angel said: "Go there yourselves and see! You will find a stable, and in the stable a baby lying in straw in a manger. He is still tiny, wrapped in bands of cloth. That baby is God's Son, who will save you!"

And all at once the angel was not alone with the shepherds. A great many more angels had come. They all praised God and shouted: "Glory to God in the highest! And on earth peace to all people who let God love them."

The shepherds listened with amazement. But when the angels had gone back to God, they didn't wait a minute longer. They said: "Let's go! Let's see this thing that God has promised!"

They left everything behind and set out for Bethlehem. And it was true: there they found Mary and Joseph and the baby in the manger. Everything was just the way the angel had said it would be.

Afterward, the shepherds went back to their sheep. But they just had to tell everyone they met on the way: "This baby will be the king of heaven and earth! He is God's Son, the one promised to us and all people. God's Son, who will save us."

They praised and thanked God for what they had heard and seen that night.

One night some Magi, people who read messages in the stars, saw a bright, shining star in the sky. They tried to find out what this sudden, blazing star meant, and they learned that it was a very special star. This star told that the king of heaven and earth had been born.

Then the Magi cried: "Look, there is the king's star!" And they started out right away to seek the newborn king. Their long caravan wound its way through Israel. In the daytime they rested, and in the night they went on. They followed the star that was showing them the way to the king.

One day the Magi came to Jerusalem, the capital city of the country. "Where can we find the newborn child?" they asked. "The baby who will be the new king. We have seen his star rising, so we came from far away in the East to honor this child and bow down to him!"

When King Herod heard this, he was afraid. No baby had been born in the royal palace. Right away Herod called his advisers, the priests and those who knew the laws and the old books, and he asked them: "Where will the king be born, the one God has promised to all people?"

The men told him what a prophet had once written: "The man who will one day lead God's people will come from Bethlehem."

So Herod sent the Magi to Bethlehem. "Go!" he said to them with a smile. "Learn everything you can about the child! And when you have found it, come and tell me! Then I, too, will go to him and bow down and honor him."

The Magi went ahead, following the star. It stopped right over the stable where Jesus lay in his manger. The men had finally reached their goal. Right away they went inside and found the baby and Mary, his mother. They knelt before him and honored him as the king whose birth God had told through the star. Then they brought in the gifts they had for him, gifts worthy of a king: gold, frankincense, and myrrh.

Later, when they were ready to return home, God spoke to them in a dream. God told them not to go home by way of Jerusalem. They must not tell Herod anything about the baby in the manger. And the Magi obeyed God.

King Herod waited a long time
for the Magi, but they never came.
All the same, he had scouts and
messengers in his service. They told
him that the child had really been
born in Bethlehem.

Herod didn't wait any longer. He
was afraid he would lose his power
and his throne. So he sent his soldiers
to Bethlehem and ordered them to
kill all the children two years old
and under.

That night, God sent an angel to
Joseph. The angel said to him in a
dream: "Get up! You have to flee to
Egypt with Mary and the baby! Hurry,
for King Herod wants to kill Jesus!"
And the angel said: "Stay in Egypt till
I tell you that you can come back!"

Then Joseph fled with Mary and the
baby, in the middle of the night. It was
a long, hard road to Egypt. But there
they were safe from Herod. Herod
could not touch God's Son.

After a few years, when the king died, Joseph and Mary went back to Nazareth with their baby. Just as before, Joseph worked as a carpenter, and Jesus grew up in Nazareth.

This book was initially published in German under the title *Jesus wird geboren* by Lahn-Verlag, Limburg, Germany. © 1995 by Lahn-Verlag, Limburg.

English-language edition © 1999 by The Order of St. Benedict, Inc., Collegeville, Minnesota, United States of America. All rights reserved. Printed in Belgium.

1	2	3	4	5	6	7	8

Library of Congress Cataloging-in-Publication Data

Krenzer, Rolf.
    [Jesus wird geboren.   English]
    Jesus is born / by Rolf Krenzer ; with Illustrations by Constanza Droop ; translation by Linda M. Maloney.
        p.   cm.
    Summary: Recounts the Biblical story of the Nativity, from the traveling of the Holy Family from Nazareth to Bethlehem, to the birth of Jesus, to his adoration by the shepherds and Magi, to the flight into Egypt.
    ISBN 0-8146-2582-7 (alk. paper)
    1. Jesus Christ—Nativity—Juvenile literature.   [1. Jesus Christ—Nativity.   2. Bible stories—N.T.]   I. Droop, Constanza, ill. II. Title.
BT315.2.K7413   1999
232.92—dc21

98-52223
CIP

but Zabel made no response, and he went on hurriedly. 'I do apologize, I really do. I didn't know you were here, of course. Rory never mentioned it. I was passing through Geneva and I just dropped by to bring him a cheese and a bottle of liqueur.'

Still Zabel said nothing. Bingham experienced a frisson of fear as the girl moved towards the bedside table, and Zabel shook his head slightly. Bingham bit his tongue. He knew he'd been babbling, and could only hope his babble had been convincing.

Finally, as the silence lengthened, Zabel said, 'Do you live in Geneva, Mr Bingham?'

'No. In Berne. And I must be off if I'm not to be too late home.'

Trina spoke for the first time. 'If you're a colleague of – of Rory's – you must work for the British Embassy, Mr Bingham?'

'Yes, that's right.' Bingham forced a smile. He had his hand on the doorknob. 'Goodbye then. My apologies once again. Tell Rory I looked in.'

Bingham heard no answer. He had shut the door and was running down the stairs, picking up his bag, leaving the house and getting into his car. He had no sense of safety till he was driving along the Rue de Haut, and he failed to notice the blue BMW that came towards him and turned into Maidment's courtyard. But Arndt Gunther had seen him drive out, and had taken a good look at him as the two cars passed each other.

★

'Why didn't you kill him, Horst?' Gunther exclaimed the moment he returned to the house and realized what had taken place. 'He'll be able to describe your new face. He'll easily recognize you again.'

'For God's sake, Arndt, think!' Zabel was worried and irritable. 'There's no reason why Bingham should associate

169

me – or Trina – with Horst Zabel, or anyone else. What does he know? Just that a couple of Maidment's friends are staying in his house and spending an afternoon in the sack. Even if he asks Maidment about us, we've still got the boy and Maidment'll take care to play ball.'

'But –'

'But, nothing! Anyway, it would have been just too bloody complex. What would we have done with his body, his car? We're getting out right now, but it would have been folly to leave Maidment his dead friend. He'd almost certainly have alerted the police, which is just what we don't want. Okay, my appearance doesn't jibe with my description, but don't forget that fool Keller and his clinic and his suicide. The authorities aren't fools, and it all fits neatly, too neatly, once they hear Maidment's story and start to put the bits together. Of course we'll kill Bingham, but at the right time and in the right city.'

'And Maidment?'

'Maidment can wait,' said Zabel. 'In the first place, we don't want the two deaths associated, and we'll probably need to fix an accident for Maidment. I'd hoped to avoid killing Maidment at all,' he went on slowly. 'If Trina and I had managed to keep away from him, and he'd eventually just gone to the authorities with a story of being forced to smuggle heroin into Switzerland to save his son, it would have been a nice red herring. But after yesterday he knows Trina, so he's got to go, too.'

'So what do we do?'

'Get out of here, cover our tracks and –'

While Zabel gave Gunther his instructions, Trina Hansen was already packing their bags, and making sure they left as few traces of their presence as possible. It was a more difficult task than leaving the Clinique de la Rocque. Their possessions now included Trina's, and it took a little time to disguise the marks on Zabel's face. But some forty minutes after Peter Bingham's departure, they were ready.

They drove straight to Cointrin. Zabel and Trina waited in one of the parking lots while Gunther went to rent a car. He came back shortly with a large Renault and, except for a bag containing a few clothes and necessities for Gunther, they transferred all their belongings from the BMW.

'We can keep the Renault as long as we like, and return it to any Avis office in Switzerland,' Gunther said, giving Trina the car's documents.

'Good.' Zabel nodded his approval. 'Trina and I'll be off then, Arndt. We'll wait for you at the hotel in Lausanne.'

'I should be with you tomorrow. If something comes up to prevent me, I'll phone.'

'Right.' Zabel got into the Renault.

'Goodbye,' Gunther said. 'Goodbye, Trina.'

'Goodbye, Arndt.'

Gunther looked at her hopefully, expecting a smile, but she was watching Zabel anxiously, aware of the strain all these rapid changes of plan were putting on him; that was why they had chosen Lausanne as their rendezvous – it was a comparatively short drive along the north shore of the lake. Gunther turned away. He got into the BMW and waited for the Renault to leave ahead of him. He sighed. He wished he were driving to Lausanne with Trina, instead of going alone to Berne to kill this Peter Bingham.

*

Rory Maidment had spent the better part of that Monday, since Hugh Cantley's return from London, closeted in the Consul-General's office. There had been plenty to discuss, major issues such as the complete reorganization of the office, as well as less important current problems. Forced to concentrate, time had passed quickly for Maidment.

When at last Cantley released him, and he returned to his own room, he was tired. Jean Rodway had already left, so automatically he tidied his desk, locked the safes and glanced at his memo pad. Peter Bingham had telephoned. He hadn't left a message, but Maidment thought he could guess the reason for the call; Peter was getting justifiably impatient.

It was late when Maidment finally reached home. He poured himself a drink and went at once to the kitchen to prepare some supper. He frowned at the large round cheese and the bottle of Kirsch on the table, then picked up the note propped against the bottle. It read: 'Will phone this evening. Mrs C.'

The meaning of the note was clear enough, but the cheese and the Kirsch remained a mystery. Were they meant as a present? A farewell gift? It seemed a little out of character for the terrorist gang. But if Mrs Carpenter hadn't left there would be no need to telephone. As the implications struck him Maidment felt his heart begin to pound against his ribs. It seemed that the crisis had come, sooner than he'd expected. He felt closer to Derek than he had for days.

Supper forgotten, he went to the garage. The blue BMW had gone. He ran into the house and up the back stairs and listened. Nothing. He walked quietly along the passage till he could see the entrance to the main bedroom suite. He had been holding his breath, and expelled it in one gasp when he saw the door was open.

The bedroom, dressing-room and bathroom were all clean, neat and tidy. The beds had been stripped and in a corner of the bathroom was a pile of dirty linen, including some of his own white shirts. The wastepaper basket was empty. There was no doubt that his unwanted guests had gone, and didn't intend to return. They had taken great pains to leave no clues to their identities or destination.

Maidment didn't care. Mrs Carpenter had left a note. She would phone with news of Derek's release. In the past she had always done as she'd promised.

He returned to the kitchen, finished his drink and made himself a sandwich. He couldn't bother with cooking now. Any moment the phone would ring.

Yet, when it did, he was slow to answer. He had immediately thought of Mrs Carpenter, but he realized it could equally well be Peter Bingham, or Geoffrey Linton.

'Hello. Maidment here,' he said warily.

'Ah, Mr Maidment! Good!' Mrs Carpenter didn't need to give her name. 'I'll be brief. We've gone, as you've no doubt discovered. Thank you for your hospitality. In return, I have to tell you that Derek will be restored to the bosom of his family, not tomorrow, but on Wednesday or possibly Thursday. We have to be practical and allow ourselves some leeway, you understand.'

'Yes. Thursday at the latest? You – you guarantee it?' In spite of himself, Maidment was aware of the absurdity of his query. 'I shan't wait any longer,' he added weakly.

'Thursday at the latest. It's a promise. Goodbye.'

Fortunately she cut the connection before Maidment could say any more – or hear her laughter.

Eighteen

Nana Smith was worried. She had received a call from the hospital that afternoon to say that she should arrange to come in on Thursday. The operation would be performed on Friday. It would be at least ten days before she could expect to be discharged.

She had nearly said she couldn't come, that she had other commitments, but she knew it would be foolish. The suggestion of a postponement could lead to another long wait, and she was getting more and more pain. She might easily collapse again, and perhaps this time the boy wouldn't stay with her.

It was a blessing when Trina telephoned. It saved her from calling the emergency number – a step she would have hated to take. Without waiting to hear Trina's message, she started to explain her problem. She spoke in German, knowing that Derek, who was having his supper in the kitchen, wouldn't understand.

Trina interrupted her. 'It doesn't matter, Nana. Just shut up the house as if you were going on holiday. We have no need for the place at the moment.'

'But the boy! What am I to do with him? I can't just leave him here.'

'Of course not.' Trina was impatient. She reminded herself that Nana was old and unwell; perhaps she was getting past her work and should be replaced. 'It's because of him I'm phoning. We've no further need of him, Nana. You can dispose of him. You know what to do.'

'Dispose of him? You don't want him set free?'

Trina made a gesture of exasperation for Zabel's benefit,

and he grinned weakly. He felt exhausted after the drive to Lausanne and the business of checking into the hotel. It was up to Trina to deal with Nana Smith.

'No, we don't want him freed, Nana. He's much too familiar with you and the house by now. It would be a risk, and one not worth taking. I know it's probably too late this evening, but tomorrow without fail, please.' It was an order, not a request.

'I understand. Tomorrow.'

Through the open door of the sitting-room Nana Smith could see into the kithen. Derek was still at the table, his fair head bowed over a plate of stew. As she watched he drank some milk, picking up the glass in both his hands. It was an endearing, childish and somehow touching action.

'Tomorrow, then,' Nana Smith repeated.

'Yes. Goodbye, Nana. I'll be in touch.'

Nana Smith replaced the receiver and returned slowly to the kitchen, her face set and stern. Derek was cleaning his plate with a piece of bread. He looked up at her, smiling.

'That was good stew. Can I have some more?'

'May I have some more, please?' She corrected him automatically, and thought at once how stupid she was to bother. After tomorrow . . . 'Yes, of course you may have some more, Derek.' Suddenly she returned his smile. 'And there's some chocolate ice cream for afters.'

While Derek ate, Nana Smith busied herself about the kitchen and thought of the next day and the order she had been given. There was really no reason why it shouldn't be carried out tonight. It wasn't very late, and it might be better to get it over. After all, she'd have plenty to do before she went into hospital, the garden to tidy, the house to clean, and it was always possible that she wouldn't return. Trina didn't seem to have thought of that. In fact, Trina had shown little interest in the operation, and had offered no sympathy.

'When I've helped you wash up, may I watch television, please?' Derek broke in on her thoughts.

'No. Yes.' Nana Smith didn't often dither. 'You can go and watch it now. I'll do the washing-up.'

'But I like to help you.' In a way this was true; to some extent Nana Smith now spelt security for Derek, or at least an element of reassurance. 'There's not much. It won't take us long,' he added, making an adult assessment.

'Very well, if you wish,' Nana Smith said tightly.

Derek looked up at her. 'Nana – is something wrong?'

'No. Why should there be?'

'I don't know, but you sound sort of – sort of funny.'

'Rubbish! If you're going to help me, hurry up, or it'll be time for bed.'

Not tonight, she decided. One more day. She was tired and her pain was troubling her. As she washed up and later watched television she thought less about the boy and more about herself. She didn't believe in an after-life, but she wasn't afraid to die. What she was suddenly facing was the knowledge that no one, not even Trina, would care one jot.

*

Death was a subject uppermost in Peter Bingham's mind, too, though not his own. He had arrived back in Berne and gone straight to the apartment block in which he lived, south of the loop in the River Aare within which the main part of the sandstone city was built, and not far from the British Embassy on the Thunstrasse. He parked his car in the underground garage, let himself into the building and took the lift direct to the top floor.

It was a fine Spring evening and from the windows of his sitting-room he could see through the trees bordering the river, past the tall spire of St Vincent's Cathedral and over the town. On a clear day one could even discern the mountains of the Swiss Jura in the background. In spite of the mediaeval charm of its arcades and fountains, Bingham often found Berne an oppressive place, and it was the view from his apartment that saved him from the occasional feeling of claustrophobia. Normally, as it grew dark, and the lights of the city came on one by one, the vista gave him great pleasure. But tonight it was different.

Tonight, like Nana Smith, he was troubled. The unexpected encounter in Maidment's house had underlined the dilemma he had been facing all the week, and he knew that he had been vacillating stupidly. He made himself a supper of scrambled eggs, cheese, some tired fruit, and ate it without interest. Then he got a can of beer from the refrigerator and took it into the larger of the two bedrooms, which he used as a studio. He got out his sketch pad and began to draw. His hobby always relaxed him, and helped him to think.

There was some excuse, he told himself, for waiting to take any action until he had returned to Berne, where his communications and best-known contacts were. But, once here, he should have gone straight to the Embassy, informed the ambassador, telexed London and set in motion the sequence of events that would lead, with any luck, to the arrest of Horst Zabel and his woman.

At least, once he'd been told that Maidment was engaged with the Consul-General, he had had enough sense not to persist with his efforts to contact him. He had realized somewhat belatedly that Zabel and the girl could only have been occupying Maidment's house with Maidment's consent, however grudging that consent might be. And, in the circumstances, while Derek was a hostage, Maidment must be regarded as no longer to be trusted. If he'd known that Bingham had identified the terrorists, he might have – probably would have – warned them.

Even now, Bingham thought, it was his personal friendship for Rory Maidment, combined with Maidment's apparently increasing involvement with the terrorists, that was restraining him from action. He had every sympathy with Rory, but could there any longer be a credible hope of saving Derek? And how much did friendship demand? Or godfathership, for that matter? There was duty to consider, too, and the other lives that sooner or later would inevitably be at risk.

Savagely Bingham tore off the top sheet of his sketch pad, crumpled it and threw it across the room. He had drawn Horst Zabel lying on the bed and Trina Hansen standing in the doorway of the bathroom. He started again, scarcely thinking of what he was doing, and found that he had reproduced the girl's face. For a moment he studied it. Then he took a fresh sheet.

He worked for some while and, when he had finished, he was pleased with the result. He was pleased also that his thoughts had clarified, and he had reached a decision – even if a negative one. He would take no action till the next day.

He would wait till Rory was in the Consulate, perhaps even phone him with spurious reassurances. Then, while Rory was in his office, his house could be surrounded and Zabel and the girl taken into custody. That way Maidment would have no reason or opportunity to warn them, and would himself be in no physical danger. As for Derek, he must take his chance; there was always a possibility – a forlorn hope, more likely – that, once in custody, the terrorists might be persuaded to release their hostage.

Bingham stood up and stretched. It had been a long, tiring day, but he felt wide awake. Useless to attempt bed; he would never sleep. What he needed was some air and exercise. The streets were well-lit and the night was fine. Why not a walk? He took an old golfing jacket from the hall cupboard, made sure he had his wallet and keys and went down in the lift.

'Going for a short stroll,' he told the porter on duty with forced cheerfulness. 'I need to stretch my legs.'

'Very good, *mein Herr*,' the man replied, returning to his newspaper. The English, he thought, were a strange people.

Bingham let himself out of the building, shut the heavy door behind him and stood for a moment on the steps, breathing in the night air. A couple of cars went by, followed by a young couple, arms around each other. He considered which way to go, and decided to make for the park bordering the river and walk through it to the famous Bärengraben – the bear-pits of Berne, home for centuries of living representatives of the city's symbol.

He set off at a fast pace and thought, like Nana Smith, 'Tomorrow. . .' Unlike Nana Smith, he wondered if Rory Maidment would ever forgive him.

★

Arndt Gunther stared in bemused surprise as Peter Bingham came out of the building. He couldn't believe his luck.

He had driven up from Geneva to Berne, had a meal in a restaurant and consulted the local telephone book. There was only one Bingham listed, complete with an address. He drove past the apartment block a couple of times, then parked where he could watch the front door. There was a light above it that illuminated all those who entered or left, and while the door was opening and shutting Gunther had been fortunate enough to spot a concierge constantly on duty at a desk in the hall.

He considered his next move. The phone book hadn't shown the number of Bingham's apartment. He could walk in boldly and ask the concierge, but the man would probably phone Bingham before admitting him, and in any case his visit would be remembered. It would be better if he could slip into the building unobserved, ring the doorbell of an apartment at random, and apologize, saying he must have been given the wrong number. He knew from experience that this ploy almost invariably produced the required information.

By now, however, it was too late for such a casual call. The concierge seemed to be immovable, and reconnaissance of the underground garage proved useless. The doors from the garage to the building itself and its lifts were firmly locked. Gunther retreated to his car. And Peter Bingham chose this moment to come out and stand on the steps of the apartment block before setting off at a brisk walk.

Gunther had seen Bingham only once, as their cars passed on the Rue de Haut back in Geneva, but he recognized him instantly. The dark curly hair and the long face were unmistakable. Gunther let him get ahead, then followed in the BMW. There was much too much light here for an attack.

When Bingham entered the park, Gunther abandoned his car and hurried after him. He was wearing crêpe-soled shoes, and made little noise. Nevertheless, Bingham became aware of someone behind him. Deliberately he slowed his pace. Berne was on the whole a law-abiding city, but there are muggers everywhere. This one was in for a surprise, Bingham thought, if he hoped for easy pickings. He swung round as Gunther came up behind him.

'Mr Bingham? Mr Peter Bingham?'

'Yes. I'm Peter Bingham. What –'

The fact that the man had addressed him by name surprised Bingham, and for a second he was off his guard. That second was enough for Gunther. He had decided on a knife, as quieter than a bullet and in skilled hands just as sure. Peter Bingham caught a glimpse of the bright metal blade and tried to twist away. He was too late. The knife was thrust deep into his body, grating against a rib, and he slid to the ground.

Gunther bent over him. He withdrew the knife, wiped it clean of blood on a paper handkerchief and threw the paper amongst the trees. He was preparing to examine the body when the shout came.

Two men in track suits were pounding towards him. What Gunther had forgotten was that, in defiance of their national reputation for hearty eating, some younger Swiss had abandoned the habits of their elders and taken to health foods and jogging. The park beside the river was a favourite spot, though not usually so late at night. Gunther turned and fled.

The two were students. At first they had seen the figures of Gunther and Bingham only as dark emerging shadows, but as they drew nearer it seemed clear to them what was happening. Without hesitation they had shouted a warning, and when Gunther made off, their suspicions were confirmed.

They visualized the attack, however, as an attempted mugging rather than an assassination, and when they reached Bingham and one of them knelt down, he was horrified, on touching the victim, to find his hand sticky with blood. He stood up, calling after his companion, but the latter was in hot pursuit of Gunther and paid no attention.

Gunther ran fast. He was in good shape and expected to outstrip his pursuer. To his annoyance he realized that he was being quickly overhauled by a younger man. He put on a spurt, but so did the man behind him. He was now outside the park, and ran past two women walking a dog as they cowered away from him. Then he heard a car behind him. A glance over his shoulder showed his pursuer in the middle of the road, waving his arms to stop it, and he saw the lighted sign 'Politzei' on its roof.

Hurriedly Gunther took the first turning that offered, then the next, and the next. He was enmeshed in a network of small streets, and suddenly found himself in a cul-de-sac. He had no idea whether his pursuers had been delayed by explanations, if they were close on his heels, or if he had lost them, but he could run no longer. He was gasping for breath, his chest heaving, and there was an almighty stitch in his side.

Ahead of him and to one side was a wall, its top only slightly higher than his head, which he guessed marked the end of someone's garden. When his breathing had become a little less harsh he took a leap, flung his arms over the wall, and somehow managed to pull himself up and on to it. In the darkness he could see the outline of a house some twenty-five yards away, and dim bushes below, but he had no choice. He let himself drop and landed heavily, twisting his right ankle.

He lay in a tangle of shrubs, waiting for a dog to start barking, for an irate householder to throw up a window, waiting . . . When he had counted to a hundred, and still neither beast nor man had shown any interest in him, he picked himself up and, keeping to the shelter of the wall, began to move in the general direction of the house.

At once an agonizing pain shot through his ankle, and he nearly cried out. After a moment he took another tentative pace or two, testing it, and found that, if he ~~were~~ _was_ careful and put little weight on his right leg, it would support him and he could manage to walk. His earlier training told him that the ankle wasn't badly broken, though he couldn't be sure about one of the small bones. At the very least, however, it was severely sprained, and needed treatment.

Treatment was the last thing it was likely to get, at least in the immediate future. Cursing to himself, Gunther set off as best he could. His progress was slow but, resting at intervals, he made it as far as the house and along a narrow passage beside it which led to a road. He had no idea where he was, but he turned left. At least walking was a little easier on the pavement than on uneven grass and he expected that, thanks to the Swiss love of neat efficiency, the road would be clearly marked at the next corner.

Gunther did not know Berne well, but he had taken the precaution of studying a street plan, and now the luck that had deserted him returned. When he reached the corner he recognized the road that ran at right angles and was able to orient himself. What was more, he realized that he must have been moving in a circle, and his car was closer than he could have hoped. Even at his slow rate of progress, it was less than fifteen minutes before he was sitting behind the wheel of the BMW.

He would have liked to rest, for movement was not improving his ankle. He had seen no sign of the police car or any police activity since he had run into the cul-de-sac and been forced to climb the wall. Nor, from where he was parked, had he any chance of seeing what was happening at the site of the attack. But he knew it would be unwise to investigate, or even stay in the vicinity of the killing. The sooner he got out of Berne and was on his way to Lausanne the better.

Nineteen

The stakes were steadily rising for all those involved, wittingly or unwittingly, with the lives of Horst Zabel and his associates.

In England Geoffrey Linton had started the day normally enough, though unusually early. It was six-thirty when he brought up early-morning tea for Julia and himself.

'As soon as I've had my tea, I'm going to phone Peter Bingham at his home number,' he said.

'At this hour?'

'Yes. Why not? It'll be getting on for eight in Berne, and if he's been away from the office for a few days he'll probably be going in early.'

'What if he says Derek's there with him?'

Linton's tone of voice dismissed such a possibility. 'I shall be very happy,' he said. Then he added, 'But I shall do my utmost to insist on speaking to the boy.'

'And if Peter says Derek's not there, but –'

Linton interrupted his wife. 'We've had enough excuses, Julia, more than enough lies. I shall contact the authorities immediately and report one missing child, and I'll pull every string I can until some real action's taken.'

Julia made no attempt to argue. She knew that Geoffrey's patience had come to an end, and she realized that his decision, unpleasant though its implications might be, was the only reasonable one. Since their conversation with Hugh Cantley on Saturday night she herself had been full of fears.

But still she remained doubtful. She compromised. 'More tea, Geoffrey?' she said.

Linton recovered from his momentary anger, and smiled at her. 'Yes, but I'll take my cup into the study, and phone from there. It's no use putting it off, darling.'

'No, of course not,' she finally acquiesced.

Julia leant back against her pillows and sipped her tea. There was a phone extension beside the bed, and she could have listened to Geoffrey's conversation with Bingham. She put out her hand towards the instrument, then drew it back. If something dreadful had happened to Derek, she thought, she would always blame herself. The details of that awful morning were still blurred in her mind, though she had tried time after time to remember every facet. But one conclusion was inevitable. Maybe she couldn't have avoided the accident, but she ought never to have let Derek go off with that strange Mrs Carpenter. One word would have been enough to stop him. A sensible woman, she knew it was useless to reproach herself, but . . .

She sat up abruptly, nearly spilling her tea, as Linton returned to the bedroom. 'Geoffrey, what is it? Tell me!' She was horrified by his expression.

Linton rubbed a hand over his unshaven chin, and hesitated before replying. 'Bad news, I'm afraid,' he said at last. 'I've been speaking to a chap from the British Embassy who answered the phone in Bingham's apartment. His name's Campbell-Rose and fortunately he'd heard of me, so he was prepared to tell me what he could. Bingham's in hospital.'

'What?'

'It seems that yesterday he got back to Berne from wherever he'd been, and in the late evening he went out for a walk. He told the porter he needed some exercise. He was attacked and knifed in a park by the river. A couple of students saw it happen and one of them chased the attacker, but he got clean away.'

'And how is Peter?'

'In intensive care. Alive, but only just. There's not a great deal of hope, according to Campbell-Rose.'

'Dear God! Poor Peter. I thought Berne was a comparatively peaceful city.'

'It is.' Linton was grim. 'They don't have many murders in the course of a year, and ordinary muggers don't usually choose a strong young man for a victim.'

Julia felt cold. 'Geoffrey, what –'

Linton shook his head. 'What am I trying to say? I don't quite know, but hasn't it occurred to you that Bingham is the third person connected with your brother to have suffered unpleasantly in the last week or so? First you, then Marie-Louise Grandin. Now Bingham. And we know that at least Bingham's attack was no accident.'

Julia didn't answer immediately, but her face mirrored her distress. 'I suppose it could be coincidence,' she said slowly. Then she added quickly. 'And Derek? We'd forgotten about Derek.'

'I hadn't. I asked the chap from the Embassy to do me a favour and ask the concierge or whoever's in charge of the building if Bingham had had anyone – any child – staying with him recently. Campbell-Rose probably thought it an odd request, but he obliged, and the answer was no. Derek's never been there, Julia.'

'Never been with Peter? You're certain?'

'Certain.'

'I see.' Julia paused while she adapted her thoughts to this new version of reality. 'So what are you going to do, Geoffrey?'

'Exactly what I said, except that I'll phone Rory first. I'll tell him about Peter Bingham, if he doesn't know already, and inform him I'm going to report his son as missing – and possibly murdered. That should make him take the situation seriously, if anything will.'

★

The telephone in Maidment's house in Geneva rang and rang. Linton was a persistent character, and he assumed his brother-in-law was asleep. But Maidment wasn't there. He was driving, foot hard down, along the Autoroute to Berne.

He had been woken AWAKENED over a couple of hours ago by Campbell-Rose. Bingham had regained consciousness, asked for Maidment and muttered something about the existence of certain sketches in his studio. Campbell-Rose had gone to Bingham's apartment, but there were a great many sketches, and none of them meant anything to him.

'Maybe they will to you,' Campbell-Rose had said over the phone. 'Anyway, Peter wants you to have them, or look at them or do something with the damned things. He did his best to emphasize their tremendous importance.'

Subduing his fears for Peter Bingham, Maidment thought about the sketches as he drove. He couldn't imagine what they might be or why he should be involved. People often muttered nonsense when they were semi-conscious, he thought. But Campbell-Rose presumably appreciated this as well as anyone, and Peter seemed to have impressed him. With a sigh Maidment dismissed his speculations and concentrated on his driving.

Traffic on the Autoroute was relatively light so early in the morning, and what there was of it – mostly large tankers and trailers – did not delay him. Maidment reached the outskirts of Berne sooner than he had expected. Here the rush hour was commencing, and Maidment stoically endured some delay caused by local congestion.

He was tempted to go straight to the hospital, but Campbell-Rose had said it would be useless – the medics had decided to operate on Bingham that morning, and there would be no news for some hours – so, with inexplicable reluctance, he made for the apartment building. The concierge was expecting him. He was shown to a visitor's parking space in the garage and escorted to Bingham's apartment.

Here the polite – almost welcoming – treatment ceased abruptly. A police officer stationed outside the door insisted that Maidment should wait until Campbell-Rose appeared. They had never met previously, but Maidment was surprised when Campbell-Rose, a thick-set, sandy-haired man with a sandy. moustache and small blue eyes set in a red face, demanded identification before allowing him into the apartment. As he rummaged in his wallet, Maidment could not avoid a mental picture of Campbell-Rose in a kilt, striding over the heather.

'Why all this security business?' Maidment asked. 'You said Peter had been mugged.'

Campbell-Rose handed back Maidment's FCO identity card and shrugged. 'There could be more to it,' he said shortly.

'I – I don't understand.'

Campbell-Rose glanced at him. 'Don't you? I gathered you and Bingham were pretty close. Surely he must have given you a hint that his job was rather different from what it appeared to be?'

Maidment paused before replying. 'Yes, I suppose he did, come to think of it,' he said carefully. In reality, he was praying: let all this be nothing to do with Derek or me.

'Bingham only came back from Germany yesterday. He has been asking questions about some nasty characters recently; it's not impossible that one of them could have followed him here. How he got on to them I've no idea. I've been after them myself without much luck, and I was hoping Bingham might help. Incidentally, I'm from the Paris Embassy – I've been attached there for the last few weeks.'

'Paris?' Once again, Maidment stared at him in surprise.

'Yes, Paris. You ever heard of someone called Horst Zabel?'

'No!' Maidment said firmly, and wondered just how much Bingham had told his colleagues. 'If he's one of these – these characters you were talking about there's no reason why I

187

should. It's not my line at all, you know. I'm a mere consul; all I do is look after lost passports.'

'I see,' said Campbell-Rose. 'Well, let's go and look at these sketches.' He made no attempt to explain his reference to Zabel.

They had been standing in the hall of the apartment, and now Campbell-Rose led the way into Bingham's studio. Without apology he went into the room first, then swung round quickly in an obvious effort to catch Maidment's reaction to the drawing pinned to a board on the easel.

His effort was in vain. Maidment had been preparing for some kind of shock, and was determined to dissemble, at least until the situation became clearer. He stared at the sketch, frowning, and after a moment, when he could trust his voice, said with perfect truth, 'I've never seen that face in my life.'

He thought he should add something, so he asked, 'Who is he?' though the question was superfluous. He knew the answer. It was the slightness of the figure that gave away the identity, rather than the lineaments of the face. Nevertheless, as Maidment studied the picture more carefully, he remembered the face of the man in the boot of his car, and could visualize the old behind the new. Coming closer to the excellent sketch, he could even perceive the faintest indications of what might be wrinkles, but could equally well have been lines of minor bruising where stitches had been removed.

Campell-Rose made no comment. He merely replaced the sketch of Zabel with one of Trina Hansen. 'What about her?' he asked abruptly.

This was merely a head and shoulders study, and Maidment regarded it with a feeling of hopelessness. If there had ever been doubt before, there was none any longer, he thought. Zabel's new face hadn't been created by Peter Bingham's imagination. Heaven knew how, but somehow Peter had seen Zabel and Mrs Carpenter – and recently.

Suddenly Maidment remembered the cheese and the bottle of liqueur on his kitchen table back in Geneva. It was typical of Peter to arrive with such gifts. Why hadn't this possibility occurred to him before? It was quite clear now what must have happened yesterday. It explained the unexpected departure of the unwanted guests – and it probably explained the attack on Peter. One of the gang had followed Peter, not from Germany, but from Geneva. No other explanation was credible.

'Well, do you know her or don't you?' Campbell-Rose was impatient.

Aware that he had been silent for too long, Maidment forced himself to grin. 'She's not a friend of mine. I wish she were. Presumably she's one of Peter's. After all, he's not married.'

Campbell-Rose didn't respond. 'I doubt if you're right,' he said. 'Take a look at this.'

It was the first sketch that Bingham had drawn. Zabel was lying on the bed, Trina, her shirt unbuttoned, was standing in a doorway. In spite of the fact that the paper was crumpled and the sketch clearly unfinished, the scene the artist had attempted to depict was apparent. And there was enough background for Maidment to identify his own bedroom.

Feigning sudden irritation, he said, 'If you've dragged me out in the middle of the night to drive up from Geneva to look at these things, you've wasted my time – and yours. You must have misheard Peter, or he was muddled about whatever he wanted to say.'

'I'm sorry.' Campbell-Rose couldn't have sounded less apologetic. 'But there could have been a connection, and I'm sure you're as keen as I am to find out who killed Bingham.'

'Killed? On the phone you said they were going to operate. He's not died since?'

'Not yet, no,' said Campbell-Rose, without any indication of sympathy.

'Christ!' Maidment said. 'I didn't realize it was as bad as

that.' He put his hands behind his back and clenched his fists to still his shaking. His thoughts mirrored those of Linton some hours ago: Julia, Marie-Louise, Peter – and Derek? He squared his shoulders. He must get back to Geneva as soon as possible; at least Mrs Carpenter and Nana Smith could locate him there.

★

To suggest that Arndt Gunther had got up early that Tuesday morning would be inaccurate. He had never been to bed. After his escape from the scene of the knifing the night before he had driven out of Berne and stopped in the first *Parkplatz* he reached. This had taken him some time. Driving with his injured ankle was a difficult and painful business.

He had known he should try to improvise a cold compress for the injury but had decided to rest first, and had made himself as comfortable as possible in one of the BMW's reclining seats. He had dozed fitfully for some fifteen minutes. Then, without warning, the reaction to his recent murderous attack and his near capture had induced a deep sleep. It was dawn before he was awakened by a blast of pop music from a station wagon that had drawn in beside him. He watched balefully as a family of five climbed out, noisily intent on breakfast.

He thought of coffee and croissants, and was suddenly hungry. He also needed to relieve himself. But walking could be a problem. He adjusted his seat to an upright position, and carefully felt his ankle. He had taken the precaution of not removing his shoe in case he was unable to replace it, and his examination showed him he had been wise. His ankle had swollen overnight, and the swelling had spread up his leg. There was little doubt that it was more than a severe sprain, and he wasn't sure that he could walk, or even drive, except perhaps with his left foot.

He opened the car door, edged himself out and stood on his

190

left leg, clinging to the car's central pillar. Gradually he shifted his weight to the right, and decided that walking was possible, just. He locked the BMW and, taking his bag with him, shuffled towards the brick multi-purpose service station nearby.

He went first to the cloakroom and washed his face. This gave him the idea of bathing his ankle, which he accomplished as well as he could without taking off his shoe. The cold water brought considerable relief, and with the help of a torn shirt he managed to improvise a tight cold compress for the affected area. Then, much more cheerful, he went along to the adjoining café.

After eating, he telephoned the hotel in Lausanne where Zabel and Trina had arranged to stay. He heard the phone ring in their room. It was answered almost immediately and Trina's voice said sharply, '*Ja? Wer* –?'

'It's me – Arndt.'

'What is it? Did you have to ring so early? You've woken Horst.'

Always Horst, Gunther thought. Be damned to Horst! He said coldly. 'It's almost nine, and I assure you it's not early as far as I'm concerned. Anyway, there are things you should know. I completed my business yesterday evening but I've had an accident –'

'With the car?'

'No, not with the car,' Gunther said irritably. 'I've sprained my bloody ankle, if not broken the damned thing, and I can hardly walk.'

'Where are you?'

'At a *Parkplatz* a few kilometres outside Berne. I think I can just about make it to Lausanne, but after that –'

'Hang on a minute.'

Gunther waited, finding more coins to feed into the telephone. He willed Trina to hurry. His ankle had started to throb, and he wanted to get back to the car. He hoped he *would* be able to drive to Lausanne. Perhaps he could pick up a hitch-hiker, who would take the wheel for him, or . . .

'Hello! Are you there?'

'Of course I'm here!' Gunther restrained his temper.

'This is very inconvenient. However, get to Lausanne as soon as you can, but don't come here. Phone when you arrive. I'll get a room for you in another hotel.'

'Right.' He heard a murmur on the line, and identified Horst's voice before the connection was cut. He sighed. Sometimes he wondered if Trina cared a damn about him. Sometimes he was certain she did not.

Twenty

Derek Maidment was having a particularly good morning. There had been eggs and bacon for breakfast, with fried mushrooms – one of his favourite dishes. Then he had been allowed into the garden. It was fine and sunny, and he had played hop-scotch on the paved path, raced around the grass and weeded one of the untidy flowerbeds.

Nana Smith had called him in for milk and chocolate biscuits at eleven, and there had been chicken for lunch. Nana was a good cook, and Derek enjoyed his food.

'Whew!' he said when he had finished his apple pie. 'That was great, Nana. I couldn't eat another crumb.'

'Good.' The old woman smiled at him, but when he grinned in return she turned abruptly away.

Derek frowned. 'Is something wrong, Nana?'

'No. Why should there be?' She replied to him as if he had been an adult, then restrained herself and began to collect the dirty dishes. 'You can help me wash up. Then you'd better have a rest.'

'Do I have to rest? You're not going out, are you, Nana?'

'No. I'm not going out. But all the same I want you in your room till tea-time,' she said firmly.

Derek sighed, but he didn't argue. 'I suppose you wouldn't let me take up the transistor?' he asked hopefully.

Nana Smith, who had planned to spend the afternoon lying on her bed listening to the radio, hesitated, then nodded. 'Yes, if you like.'

'Thank you. And you won't lock me in?'

'Not if you promise to stay in your room.' Nana Smith had

started to wash the dishes. 'Anything else you'd like?'

She had meant it as a teasing remark, but regretted it when she saw the boy's face cloud over. She guessed what was passing through his mind. Poor child, she thought. It wasn't his fault, none of it. Why should he have to suffer? She sighed. In spite of her background she had never liked making use of children.

'It's Tuesday today, isn't it?' Derek asked suddenly.

'Yes. Why?'

'If things had been – different, I'd have been coming home from Switzerland tomorrow, and Aunt Julia would have been driving me back to school on Thursday. That won't happen now, will it, Nana?'

'I wouldn't imagine so.'

'But I'm not going to stay here with you for always, am I?'

Nana Smith heard the tears in his voice, and said at once, 'Of course you're not, Derek. In fact . . .' She hesitated. She couldn't tell him the truth, that this was the last day he would be spending with her. 'In fact, I wouldn't be surprised if you weren't free of me quite soon.'

'Oh, Nana, I didn't mean it like that. It – it's just that it's not home.'

'I know, Derek.' Nana Smith smiled at him. 'Off you go then. Don't forget to take the wireless. If you're a good boy I'll let you stay up late and watch the telly. There's a magic show tonight, I think.'

Derek slowly climbed the stairs to the attic room he now thought of as his own. He was puzzled. Nana was often kind and gave him small treats, but he had never before known her to be quite so indulgent as today. Her attitude worried him, though he couldn't have explained why.

He lay on his bed and fiddled with the transistor radio. Most of the time he listened to music, but in the course of the afternoon there was a newsflash. The President of France, who had been grievously ill since the terrorist attack on his life, had died. The hunt for those responsible for the assassination had been widened, as it was now believed that they had managed to leave France.

Derek knew about the attack. He had heard his Uncle Geoffrey speak of it, and had seen headlines in the newspapers. His interest had been slight. Now, hearing of the President's death, he felt vaguely sorry, but as the newscaster continued with a short obituary, he switched to another station. It never occurred to him that his own expectation of life was in any way related to the manhunt for the President's killer.

★

Rory Maidment heard the news of the President's death on his car radio as he was leaving Berne and, unlike his son, continued to listen, promptly tuning to a French station. He heard a lengthy eulogy, stressing the dead man's contribution to his country's well-being, and a respectful expression of condolence to the late President's family. Then a collection of pundits began to speak about wider issues.

The President, they agreed, had been a stabilizing factor in the French Republic, keeping a nice balance between right and left. With his demise, the balance would be upset, coalitions would split and the political pendulum would almost certainly swing leftwards. This, it was argued, might well be dangerous, if not disastrous, not only for France itself, but for the West as a whole. The effects of the assassination could prove to be of long-term significance, especially as the terrorists who had planned and executed it – and probably other previous operations – were still at large, representing a continuing threat.

Maidment wiped a hand across his eyes. It was tears, not rain on the windshield, that were blurring his vision, he realized. He drew off the highway on to the shoulder, hunched his arms over the steering-wheel, and buried his face in them. He wept openly. It was several minutes before he was in full control of his feelings.

He couldn't explain why his spirit had broken at this point. He had no personal feelings about the French President, and he was inclined to take some of the more sinister implications of the man's death as expressed by the national commentators as merely typical exaggeration of the importance of France's place on the international scene. Perhaps, he thought, his unexpected breakdown had been due to a sudden appreciation of his own position – a realization of how far he himself had entered into an unholy alliance with the terrorists. And what, he asked himself, had he to show for his cooperation? Was there any realistic basis for a belief that he would ever see Derek alive again?

Maidment wiped his eyes and blew his nose. He started the engine and edged the Jaguar back into the traffic stream. His reflections had changed his mind. The office could do without him for the rest of the day and, as for Mrs Carpenter, if she wanted him she could try later. He would go direct to Annecy. He had neglected Marie-Louise for far too long, and he had a sudden urge to be with her.

He found her with old Grandin in a sheltered corner of their garden, enjoying the sunshine. They were surprised to see him, but welcoming. He shook hands with Denis, and knelt down beside the chaise-longue to kiss Marie-Louise.

'You have news of Derek?' she asked at once, holding him and looking anxiously into his face.

Maidment shook his head, reproaching himself as he saw her pallor and the dark circles under her eyes. He blamed himself bitterly for what had happened to her, but at least she had survived and would suffer no long-term harm; and she was young, still young enough to have children, he thought. But how could he visualize himself marrying again and raising a family? Surely the ghost of Derek would always come between him and them?

He said, 'Not really. I've spoken to him a couple of times on the phone. He sounded well, and as cheerful as one could expect.'

'I don't understand it,' Grandin said. 'You've done all that this gang asked of you, but they have neither released the boy, nor, as far as we know, killed him.' He paused, realizing how bluntly he had spoken, but went on when Maidment showed no reaction. 'Has there been any hint they want you to carry anything else across the border?'

'None at all,' Maidment said, and thought regretfully of the great gaps in the Grandins' knowledge of events – gaps that it was now too late to fill. He was beginning to think that coming to Annecy had been a mistake.

He saw Denis watching him curiously, and hastened to add, 'The last thing they told me was that they needed time – perhaps to distribute the stuff – but Derek would be set free this week.'

'Then there is hope.' Marie-Louise's face lit up.

'Yes,' Maidment agreed, though he wasn't sure that he believed it any longer.

He changed the subject, asking Marie-Louise how she was. He was duly solicitous, but when Denis Grandin made a tactful attempt to leave him alone with Marie-Louise he said immediately that he couldn't stay long, that he would like an early aperitif, and then must leave for Geneva.

Father and daughter exchanged glances, but said nothing. Maidment drank his whisky, and inevitably the conversation turned to the death of the President. Grandin seemed eager to discuss the implications for France and the Western world but Maidment, conscious of Marie-Louise's eyes upon him, contributed little. He was thankful when he could decently depart.

He would not have been so thankful if he had heard Grandin's remark as his car drove away. 'I'm sorry, *chérie*, but in all conscience I can wait no longer. Rory, I'm sure, is deceiving us. I intend to use my contacts to get in touch with the security authorities – the DST, I think, rather than the police.'

★

It was a laborious drive from Berne to Lausanne for Arndt Gunther. The pain in his ankle nagged at him continuously and he was forced to make innumerable stops. He was fond of opera, and his only distraction came from the tape cassettes he played continuously. It was because of these that he arrived at his destination still in ignorance of the President's death.

By the time he got to Lausanne he was in no mood to find a telephone and call Trina as she had instructed him. He made straight for the hotel where she and Zabel were staying, thankfully gave the keys of the BMW to the concierge, and hobbled to the reception desk. The receptionist was understanding; he found Gunther a single room, lent him a walking stick which a previous guest had left behind and suggested the hotel's doctor. Gunther hesitated, then agreed. A doctor would probably insist on an X-ray, but even without this would provide proper strapping and some powerful painkillers.

Grimacing with pain, Gunther sat on his bed and gingerly took off his right shoe. His leg was swollen up to and beyond the knee, and it throbbed steadily. He debated whether to wait for the doctor before phoning Trina, but decided against any delay. The doctor could well be some time in arriving, and Trina would be waiting to hear from him.

He punched out the room number that Trina had given him, and the phone was picked up immediately. Gunther didn't announce himself. He said, 'I'm here, in Room 28.'

'But I told you –'

'I know what you told me, but I'm in no state to mess about. I can barely walk. My ankle – my whole leg – has puffed up like a balloon. I suspect I've fractured a small bone.'

'So you're useless.' It was an accusatsion.

'It depends what for. My brain's still working,' Gunther

198

snapped.

'Not very well,' retorted Trina. 'Or haven't you heard the news? And don't say, "What news?"'

Gunther had been about to ask just that, and restrained himself with difficulty. Somehow Trina always managed to get the best of any discussion.

'So what do you want me to do? I'm waiting for a doctor, but –'

'A doctor?' Trina interrupted. 'All right. I shall come to your room – when we have reconsidered the situation.'

In the event the doctor arrived first. A short, dapper Swiss, he was competent and practical. He appreciated that his patient wanted to get home – Zurich was indeed a beautiful city – and wouldn't wish to be bothered with hospitals and X-rays in Lausanne. So all he could do was prescribe rest, cold compresses, painkillers and, if weight must be put on the damaged ankle, a strong supportive bandage and a stick. As for driving, that was out of the question – dangerous, if not impossible, even with automatic transmission. Doubtless suitable arrangements could be made about the car.

When the doctor had gone Gunther swore. He was feeling considerably more comfortable, and the pain had eased, but it was a miserable fact that, as Trina had said, he was useless. The car was of no consequence. He could arrange for it to be left in a long-term car park, and abandoned. But if he really were unable to drive . . .

While he waited for Trina he turned on the television, and thus learnt for the first time that the French President had succumbed to his wounds. The news cheered but also puzzled him. The brief conversation he'd had with Trina had left him with the impression that the news she'd mentioned was the reverse of good.

He switched off the set as there was a triple knock on the door, swung himself off the bed, and limped across the room to let Trina in. Her face told him nothing, but he sensed that she was tense and purposeful.

199

'It's great about the Frenchman, yes?' he said.

'Sure.' Trina threw herself into a chair. 'It's a pity the rest of the news isn't so good.'

'Meaning?' Gunther was alert.

'They know the man they want has got out of France. That was on the radio, and as a result I've been in touch with some of our people in Germany. There's gossip the killer's been smuggled into Switzerland. What's more, the name Horst Zabel's been mentioned, so we can assume the connection's been made. Horst's not safe in this country any more, Arndt.'

'No one would recognize him now.'

'He's not safe here,' Trina repeated firmly. 'These are just the rumours. You can bet the authorities know a hell of a lot more.'

'Maidment?'

'Possibly, though probably not intentionally. That brother-in-law of his, Linton, perhaps. But how's not important. Horst wants to leave as soon as possible. He says he's quite well enough to go straight through to the GDR. We'd leave right away, but someone's got to deal with Maidment. If you'd not had this stupid accident –'

'You don't even know how I hurt myself.'

'It doesn't matter. I'll take the BMW and cope with Maidment this evening when he's sure to be home. There'll be no problems. He'll think I've come to tell him about that son of his. You've still got the key to his house, haven't you?' Gunther nodded. 'Fine. I'll get back here as soon as I can, but while I'm gone I want you to stay with Horst. Okay?'

'Yes. And tomorrow?'

'We shall start early, Horst and I. You'll have to make your own way, Arndt. Report in when you arrive.'

'Right,' Gunther said. He made no attempt to argue. He knew it would be pointless.

★

At tea-time Derek told Nana Smith about the President's death, but she was indifferent. She had no knowledge of Zabel's operation, and in any case had other things on her mind. Her edginess communicated itself to Derek who, as the day progressed, had lost most of the exuberance he had felt during the morning. At supper they were both unusually silent. Nana Smith seemed so preoccupied with her own thoughts that Derek began to wonder if she was unwell again.

But after the meal had been cleared away she didn't send him to bed early, as he had half-expected. She said he could look at television, and later she brought him a hot chocolate drink, which she knew he liked. She watched him as he drank, her face expressionless, even when he put down the glass, leaving a wide chocolate mark around his childish lips – a sight which would have touched almost anyone.

Twenty minutes later Derek began to feel drowsy. His head nodded, the screen blurred and he tried to jerk himself awake. In a little while he was fast asleep. Nana Smith waited. She was determined that the boy should not be frightened unnecessarily. When she was certain the drug she had given him had taken hold and he wouldn't reawaken suddenly, she went up to the attic room, packed his clothes and possessions, and got herself ready.

It was dark when she wrapped Derek's slight body in a rug, carried him out to her car and laid him on the back seat. She locked the house and drove off. Tomorrow, she thought sadly, she would have to clean his room, and remove all signs of his presence. Meanwhile she had a long drive ahead of her.

Twenty-one

Trina left Lausanne for Geneva later than she had intended. Zabel had ordered dinner sent up to their room, and then had wanted her to come to bed. At first a little reluctant, she took off the dark slacks, shirt and jacket she intended to wear for her mission. Later, she dressed quickly after a hasty shower, checked her Makarov pistol, phoned Gunther to say she was leaving and, without waiting for him to come and join Horst, went down to collect the BMW.

She drove fast, keeping the window beside her partly open. The rush of cold night air exhilarated her – that and the thought of killing. Zabel, she knew, would have preferred Maidment's death to appear an accident, but there was now no time for such refinements. She would shoot on sight.

Reaching the old town she drove straight along the Rue de Haut and turned into Maidment's courtyard. If anyone noticed the car and remembered it later, it wouldn't matter; the BMW would be abandoned tomorrow. She parked, switched off the engine and sat still for a moment, staring at the house. It was in darkness. Either Maidment was not at home, which was unlikely as he would surely be eagerly waiting to hear from her, or he had gone to bed.

Trina got out of the car quietly, and shut its door without a sound. If Maidment really was asleep, there was no need to wake him prematurely. The moon was in its third quarter, and when it came out from behind cloud there was adequate light for her to fit the front door key easily into the lock. She opened the door carefully, stepped inside the house and listened.

A clock ticking, a beam creaking, the sharp crack of old wood expanding, but nothing inexplicable or alarming. Finally confident, Trina shut the front door behind her. Then she picked her way carefully up the stairs and without hesitation turned towards the room where Maidment had slept when Zabel was in the house. The chances were he wouldn't yet have reoccupied his old bedroom.

The door was ajar. She pushed at it gently, her pistol already in her hand, and smiled to herself as she saw the outline of Maidment's body hunched under the duvet, his back to her. But momentarily scattered cloud passed across the face of the moon and the room grew dim, so that she paused on the threshold. Then as the light brightened again, she moved forward, glancing neither to right nor left.

That was her mistake. She heard no sound. Rather she sensed her danger, but too late to take evasive action. She was aware of a dark shadow beside her, an upraised arm. Then something heavy descended on her head, seeming to split her skull, and she plunged into blackness and fell forwards.

Maidment jumped over the still form on the floor, grabbed the pistol and switched on the light. 'Christ!' he muttered as he identified his victim. He hadn't expected his visitor to be *Mrs* Carpenter.

Unable to sleep, Maidment had been sitting in darkness by the bedroom window when the BMW turned into the courtyard. He had recognized the car instantly, but he had caught only a glimpse of the dark, trousered figure who got out of it and had assumed it was the man he thought of as Mr Carpenter. Straining his ears, he had heard the front door open, and then, after a silent pause, the unmistakable creak of a stair.

Afterwards he was not sure why – the care with which the intruder was moving, perhaps – but Maidment immediately assumed the existence of a threat. He acted as swiftly and silently as he could, bunching up his pillows on his bed and pulling the duvet over them. Then he looked around for a weapon, seized a heavy brass candlestick, flattened himself against the wall beside the door and waited.

That the figure he'd hit was a woman – Mrs Carpenter – had surprised Maidment, but caused him no remorse. Quite apart from her surreptitious entry, the gun he had seen in her hand was sufficient evidence of the danger he'd been faced with. He, like Peter and the others, was expendable – and that had to include Derek. He had been a fool not to accept this before.

Now he treated Trina's unconscious body without the least compassion. Some of his neckties were immediately available and he used these to bind her hands behind her, and her ankles. Then he lifted her on to a high straight-backed chair and, ripping the electric flex from a bedside lamp used that, with more neckties, to secure her in a sitting position. It was an amateur job, but he did his best to ensure it was efficient.

By the time he had finished and seated himself on the bed opposite her and a few feet away, Trina was beginning to regain consciousness. Her lids fluttered as she opened her eyes. Then she slowly lifted her head. She could feel blood from a wound trickling down one cheek. She glared at Maidment.

He said, 'Mrs Carpenter, I don't intend to kill you, though I must admit I'm tempted. But I suspect you'd prefer it to a long term in prison – which is your only alternative.'

Trina said nothing. Her head was aching violently and she was furious at herself for having been trapped so easily. She forced her mind to work and made an abortive effort to test the strength of her bonds. Then she suddenly relaxed. If she were to escape from her present situation, clearly it would be through guile rather than force.

'First, I want some answers.' Maidment was watching her closely. 'What have you done with Derek?'

'What we promised, Mr Maidment.' Trina answered after only a momentary hesitation. 'We intend that tomorrow Nana Smith will drive him from her house into London, and drop him outside Hampstead Underground Station. But there's a catch. She won't do this unless I order her to.'

She knew as she spoke that the ploy was too simple. For a second hope flickered in Maidment's mind, only to be instantly rejected. The woman had come to shoot him while he slept. And if him, why not Derek?

'And where's Derek now? Where's this house of Nana Smith's?'

'In the country, not too far from London.'

'Where, exactly? It'll be found, you know, sooner or later. The police will find it. After all, I've learnt a certain amount about it – its isolation, its walled garden, the old woman who was once a children's nanny.'

'So what? You couldn't identify Nana Smith or the house; you've never seen either of them.' Trina was scornful, unaware that she had finally confirmed Maidment's worst fears.

'Derek could, Mrs Carpenter,' he said quietly. 'Just as I could identify you and your chum, whoever he is. Just as Peter Bingham can identify Horst Zabel's new face. Which is why you need us all dead if you're to cover your tracks completely. It's pretty obvious, isn't it?'

Trina stared at him, her chest rising and falling rapidly. She was appalled. Nana, the house, Gunther – none of them mattered. She herself didn't matter. But Horst . . . How did Maidment know about Horst? Gunther was supposed to have killed Bingham.

'Peter Bingham *can* –' she said involuntarily.

But Maidment was already reading her thoughts. He said, 'Peter Bingham isn't dead yet, you'll be glad to know. You bungled the job. I was talking to the hospital in Berne earlier and he's survived an operation satisfactorily. What's more, I expect you knew he was an artist, and a good one. Well, before he was attacked he drew some wonderful likenesses of you, and of your colleague with that new face Dr Keller gave him at the Clinique de la Rocque.'

This was when Trina Hansen began to feel real fear, not only for Horst Zabel, but for herself. She didn't understand Maidment in this mood – determined, almost mocking, sure he had nothing to lose. Perhaps, in spite of his words, he did intend to kill her – he might think it a revenge for the agony he had been through – and she didn't want to die. But she would never try to save herself by betraying Horst.

'And where is Horst Zabel?' Maidment demanded abruptly, once more as if in answer to her thoughts.

'Where none of you will find him.'

'Where is he?' Maidment asked again, disregarding Trina's reply. He lifted her gun. 'Where is he? And where's the other man – Mr Carpenter, if that's his name? Answer me!'

'Or you'll shoot? Okay, go ahead, shoot!' She would have given him Gunther to save herself, but that was impossible without leading him to Horst. 'Shoot!' she repeated. 'Or don't you have the guts, Mr Maidment?'

Trina Hansen misjudged Maidment. He would have shot her without a qualm, but she alone was not enough. To repay the debt they owed him he must have them all – the two Carpenters and Nana Smith, and especially Horst Zabel. He realized the terrorist quartet couldn't be alone; there had to be other accomplices in the background, but these were none of his personal concern. Nothing would bring Derek back, nothing would undo what had been done, but at least the arrest of these four would be compensation of a sort.

Deliberately Maidment dropped the pistol on the bed, stood up and took one step towards Trina. Suddenly he hit her with the back of his hand across the face one way, then with his palm the other. As the wound in her head smashed against the chair, the girl screamed and blacked out, falling forwards against her bonds.

She regained consciousness a few moments later, to find Maidment kneeling beside her, his hands on her body, in her pockets. As she squirmed at his touch he quickly rose to his feet, clutching the object he had found in the left hand pocket of her slacks. He held it up so that she could see it, and was rewarded by an expression of horror that she failed to hide. It was a hotel room key, attached to a metal plate. She had taken it with her when she went to talk to Gunther, and later had forgotten to leave it with Zabel. She tried to remember what was on the plate.

Maidment enlightened her. 'Hôtel d'Esterre, Lausanne. Room 37,' he read. 'So that's where you're staying? You and Horst Zabel? And Mr Carpenter?' He grinned at her and, with a flash of inspiration, added, 'I'll make sure Zabel knows you told me where to find him.'

It was too much for Trina. She could contain herself no longer. 'You'll never see your son again,' she screamed at Maidment. 'He's dead, dead!' And, as Maidment looked at her with loathing, she collected a gob of spittle in her mouth and, leaning forward as far as she could, spat in his face.

In a sense Maidment had already discounted the fact that his son was dead, but this sudden confirmation was overwhelming. Slowly he reached for a handkerchief and wiped the spittle off his cheek. Then, without a word, he switched off the light and left the room. He hadn't bothered to gag her, knowing there was no one to hear her shouts, and he was followed by a stream of abuse in gutter German, most of which he failed to understand. Five minutes later Trina heard him get his car out of the garage and drive off. She wept tears of anger and frustration as she began to struggle fruitlessly to free herself. If only she could warn Horst, she thought, perhaps he'd have a chance to get away. But how could she manage this?

*

As Maidment set off for Lausanne, Nana Smith was reaching north London. She was making for Hampstead, but for the Heath, not the Underground Station. It was an area she had once known well, for she had spent some years as nanny to the children of an exotic couple – he a Member of Parliament, she an actress – who had treated her as one of the family but, she remembered, often forgotten to pay her.

She recalled the children, two girls and a boy, though she had lost touch with them long ago. The boy had been very like Derek Maidment, with the same fair hair and appealing brown eyes. Idly, as she drove automatically, she wondered what had happened to him, if he had been luckier than young Derek.

Stopped at traffic lights, she looked quickly over her shoulder, fearful that an arm might be hanging out or the face had become uncovered. But the still bundle remained securely wrapped in its rug. Nana Smith sighed heavily. The lights changed and she moved on, passing not far from the house where Geoffrey and Julia Linton were preparing for bed.

She missed one turning, but soon found her way again and drew up at the end of a narrow road on the edge of the Heath. For a minute she sat at the wheel, bracing herself for what she was about to do. It was dark, the backs of the few nearby houses showing no lights, and Nana Smith shivered as she got out of the car, once more conscious of her pain.

There was a pond not far away, and she intended to throw Derek and his bag into the water. She took the bag first. It seemed to have grown heavier during the journey, and she decided not to bother with it. She pushed it under the first convenient bush she came across and paused, panting, before she went back for the boy.

His body, though small, was seemingly as heavy as the bag, and more difficult to lift out of the car. Then somewhere near a dog barked, startling Nana Smith and causing her to glance around anxiously. It was a false alarm; no one seemed to be about, but her sudden movement had caused the rug to slip from Derek's face. Hurriedly she covered it again; she didn't want to look at him or think about what she planned to do. Stupidly she had let herself become fond of the child.

For a few yards she struggled with him over the rough grass, but her pain was now intense, coming over her in waves. She knew she was never going to reach the pond. As she collapsed with Derek in her arms, she was suddenly glad that her problem was to be solved for her. She died while Derek slept.

★

Trina Hansen continued to struggle fitfully, but Maidment had tied her securely and she was achieving nothing. Suddenly, as she realized how time was passing, she indulged her frustration by a burst of frantic activity. She started to rock from side to side, regardless of any risk to herself, and eventually she was rewarded. A wooden leg broke as the chair fell violently sideways.

She hit the floor heavily and for a moment was stunned again. Then she realized that the rung of the chair to which her legs were tied was also broken and her ankles were free, though still bound together. After some experiments she discovered that she was able to propel herself along the ground on her side, though still secured to her chair and with the utmost difficulty. Rejoicing that Maidment had failed to gag her, she began the long, painful journey to the main bedroom suite at the far end of the corridor. She knew there was a telephone there, and she hoped that somehow she could find a way to use it.

Twenty-two

Rory Maidment was not a stupid man. In spite of the pressures upon him, he had not set off for Lausanne in a blind surge of emotion, but with relative calm and purposefully. Derek was dead; he accepted that. Later, he would grieve properly for his son. Now he had a job to do, and he knew he must approach it sensibly.

His first instinct, when he had discovered Horst Zabel's whereabouts, had been to call the authorities, but he rejected that idea as soon as he thought of it. He had no direct contacts with the Swiss security and intelligence services; indeed, his only contacts with the ordinary police had been on the level of lost passports or travellers' cheques. There was no senior officer to whom he could appeal on a personal basis in the hope of being taken seriously.

And even if he did have a suitable contact, explanations would inevitably be tortuous. An attractive young woman, said to have kidnapped his son, and now to be found tied to a chair in a bedroom of his house in Geneva? Two guests in a presumably reputable hotel in Lausanne: one the assassin of the President of France, except that his face failed to correspond with the official pictures spread across Europe, the other wanted for the attempted murder of a British diplomat in Berne? Who would believe such tales without lengthy inquiry?

Letting his Jaguar out on the Autoroute to Lausanne, Maidment perceived he had a problem. With Peter Bingham's survival still in doubt, much of the evidence against Zabel and the Carpenters was known only to himself, and if anything should happen to him . . . He had no illusions that the terrorists would willingly surrender and, though he was prepared to use Mrs Carpenter's pistol, the confrontation could be dangerous.

Maidment resented the inevitable delay, but forced himself to stop at an *Aire de service* on the outskirts of Lausanne, and find a telephone. He called the number that Campbell-Rose had insisted he should take, and listened anxiously to the ringing tone from Berne. It seemed to him an age before a sleepy voice answered.

'Campbell-Rose speaking.'

'Maidment. Rory Maidment. I'm using a public phone. I haven't got much change, and this may take a while. Call me back right away. It's important. And get ready to take notes.' Maidment gave the number on the instrument before him.

'Okay.' The voice had lost its sleepiness.

It was only seconds before the phone rang. Campbell-Rose's voice said, 'Right. Spill it. I'm recording.'

Maidment found it difficult to know where to begin. He said, 'I lied to you this morning. Those sketches Peter made. The man is Horst Zabel. I brought him into Switzerland in the boot of my car.'

Campbell-Rose hid any surprise he was feeling. 'Go on,' he said calmly.

Maidment did his best, trying to keep to essentials and avoiding explanations. He found Campbell-Rose a good listener, expressing neither condemnation nor sympathy. The questions he asked were pertinent. Altogether, he gave Maidment confidence.

'Fine,' Campbell-Rose said at last. 'Leave it to me. I know the chaps to call. With any luck we'll get Zabel this time.'

'I'll be at the hotel.'

'No! Stay where you are. Or – better still – go home. Your Mrs Carpenter will have been collected by the time you get back.'

'I'll be at the hotel,' Maidment repeated and put down the

receiver, giving Campbell-Rose no chance to argue. He was most certainly not going to wait tamely at home until officialdom arrived to question him, and tell him what they thought he ought to know. He had a personal interest in this conflict. Besides, he didn't altogether share Campbell-Rose's apparent faith that his 'chaps' would accept the story and act on it with sufficient speed. There had been enough delays already; Zabel must surely be feeling the first prickings of anxiety at having heard no word from Mrs Carpenter.

On his way out of the service area, Maidment asked for directions to the Hôtel d'Esterre in the city. This provoked some discussion and a search of the local hotel directory. More precious minutes were wasted, but at last Maidment was sure he knew where to go. He ran for his car. However efficient Campbell-Rose might be, he still expected to reach the hotel before the police or the security services, and he felt an icy pleasure at the thought of meeting Horst Zabel.

★

Trina Hansen was also thinking of Horst Zabel, but her thoughts were very different from those of the man who had outwitted her. She hadn't spared herself. Crawling, half-rising to stagger a couple of feet, falling and lying exhausted, she had more than once blacked out completely. But she persevered, determined to reach the telephone.

She was sobbing from the pain of her head wound and the bruising from her falls when she came at last to the end of the corridor. Here she paused for a brief respite in the doorway of the bedroom suite. She could see the phone on the bedside table. One final effort, and it was within her reach.

Or it would have been, she thought bitterly, if her hands were not bound behind her back, and her body attached to this bloody chair. Then she realized that her painful struggle along the passage had had some advantages. Some of the neckties had stretched or loosened, and the chair, never intended for such treatment, was on the verge of coming apart in several places. It took a lot more effort and a lot more pain, but eventually she was able to slide her wrists and ankles over the shattered ends of wood, and free herself from her burden.

Her hands were bleeding and full of splinters but she didn't care. She lay on her side on the floor and, straining every muscle, managed by a series of contortions to pass her feet between her arms over the necktie that bound her wrists behind her back. A final violent jerk and she had succeeded. Her hands were now in front of her.

She had to rest again though she, too, was worried about time – the time she had taken to reach her goal and the time she had wasted in efforts to free herself before her chair had tipped sideways. She pictured Maidment in Lausanne, bursting into Room 37 at the Hôtel d'Esterre and catching Horst unawares, shooting him perhaps – and with her gun – before he had a chance. Slowly she pulled herself upright and sat on the edge of the bed.

In common with most modern telephones in Switzerland, the instrument had a keypad rather than a dial, and even with bound wrists Trina found no difficulty in punching out the number. She willed Zabel to reply quickly, but to her annoyance it was Gunther who answered with a cautious, 'Hello.'

'Horst! Let me speak to Horst!'

'He's in the bathroom,' Gunther replied automatically, but the urgency in Trina's voice had communicated itself to him. 'Trina, what is it? Something wrong?'

'Yes. Maidment tricked me, knocked me out. He found the hotel key in my pocket and he's on his way now, probably with the police. He knows almost everything – and he can recognize Horst.'

'Recognize Horst? But –'

'Don't argue. Just get Horst out of there at once! Don't you understand, Arndt? Horst's in danger.' She added some

213

words which jolted Gunther; Trina only relapsed into obscenities in times of real crisis.

'Okay. But what about you? Where shall we meet?'

'Forget me. Just make sure that Horst gets away before –'

'Trina!' Her voice was fading, and Gunther was thoroughly alarmed. 'Where are you? Are you hurt?'

'Maidment's house. He split my head open.'

'What is it?' Zabel had returned from the bathroom.

'I'll come and get you, Trina. I'll be there as soon as –'

'No! No, Arndt!' She was screaming at him in her effort to impose her will. 'Look after Horst. He's not strong enough yet to cope by himself. He must go, get away immediately – and you must help him.'

'Let me talk to her,' Zabel said, taking the receiver from Gunther. 'Trina, this is Horst. Trina?'

But there was no answer, though the line was still open. Trina, dropping the phone, had fallen back on to the bed unconscious, a slight smile on her lips. She had succeeded in warning Horst, and that was all that mattered.

Zabel turned on Gunther. 'Something's happened to her. What did she say?'

'Maidment't hurt her, badly, I think. And he knows where we are – and he can recognize you. We can expect him – and the fuzz – any minute.'

Gunther was already making plans, his mind intent on getting to Trina. He tried his ankle tentatively. The few hours' rest had improved it, but it was still incapacitating. He would never be able to drive to Geneva. He would have to hire a car with a driver, or take the Renault and pay or force someone to drive it. He was scarcely aware of Zabel.

For his part, Zabel had been getting ready for bed. He had spent much of the day dozing, but the need for sex and its satisfaction had tired him once again. He had been looking forward to a good night's sleep. Now, because Trina had bungled the Maidment job, he was being compelled to flee in desperate circumstances. Silently cursing, he pulled off his pyjamas and began to dress.

'We'll take the Renault, but get rid of it as soon as possible,' he said decisively. 'The hotel could identify it. You'll have to get another car.'

'I can't drive, not far, if at all.'

'Then I'll have to,' Zabel snapped, though he hated being trapped behind the wheel of a car. 'We'll head for Zurich as we planned, not that we want to stay there. But it's got an airport, and it's near the German border. It's imperative we get out of Switzerland.'

Gunther stared at him. 'What about Trina?' he asked slowly.

'What about her?'

'We can't just abandon her like – like a car that's hot. She's in Maidment's house, injured while doing a job to cover for you.'

'A job you should have been doing, Arndt,' Zabel said coldly. 'And she seems to have made a mess of it.'

'So you'll leave her.'

'Of course. Fetch what you want from your room and let's get going. We'll meet in the lobby. Hurry!'

Zabel was acting in accordance with one of the unwritten rules of the group. No single member should needlessly break his cover or sacrifice himself for another. Gunther had never questioned it before, any more than he had questioned Zabel's authority. But Trina was different – and till now he had believed that Zabel also thought her an exception. She was, after all, his acknowledged second-in-command, and it was due to her that Zabel had been saved from the French. And all this apart from any personal relationship . . . Gunther shut his eyes.

'I'm going to Geneva,' he said at last. 'There must be something I can do for her.'

'Don't be so bloody stupid! *I* need you.' The voice of command was obvious. 'Two of us'll have fifty times the chance of one alone.'

Zabel was at the door, a small bag in his hand. 'Come on,' he said urgently. He was used to unquestioning obedience, and it didn't occur to him that Gunther's protest was to be taken seriously. He glanced around the room, switched out the light and stepped into the corridor. He felt Gunther's hand on his arm.

'I mean it, Horst. I'm going to Geneva.'

The events of the next few seconds were confused. Some fifteen yards along the corridor the doors of the lift sighed open and a man got out. To Zabel Rory Maidment was a total stranger. Gunther, in the doorway behind Zabel, had no means of seeing who it was. But Maidment recognized Zabel. He gripped Trina's Makarov and pulled it from his pocket.

Zabel's reactions were rapid, automatic. One moment he had no pistol, the next he had fired a shot. It was inevitably hasty, but Zabel was a brilliant marksman. The only thing that saved Maidment from instant death was the fact that Gunther sensed a crisis and involuntarily tightened his grip on Zabel's arm, disturbing his balance.

As it was, the bullet caught Maidment in the shoulder. He felt no pain immediately, but was knocked backwards against the edge of the open lift with considerable force. Somehow he managed to keep hold of his gun, but the shot that he loosed off went harmlessly into the plasterwork of the ceiling.

Zabel, under the impression that Gunther was attempting to restrain him, kicked back viciously, making contact with Gunther's injured ankle. Gunther shouted in agony, staggered and fell. Zabel ran for the service stairs.

Unfortunately for him, the stairs were at the furthest end of the corridor, beyond the lifts, and by the time Zabel had reached the fire door Maidment had heaved himself upright. It was much too late to attempt another shot but, regardless of the blood soaking the front of his shirt and the sudden awareness of pain, Maidment found himself, teeth gritted, running, staggering, in pursuit.

Zabel arrived on the ground floor, breathing hard. It was weeks since he had taken any physical exercise. Indeed, the last time he had exerted himself in any way was when he had been forced to flee from the French police after shooting their President. That had been a close call. It was only due to Trina's quick wits and a diversion created by Gunther that he had escaped from *les flics*. This time things were different; he was alone and he was weak.

Forced to rest for a moment Zabel heard hasty footsteps on the concrete stairs above him. Glancing up the well, he saw the man who had pulled a gun on him coming down. He had no doubt that it was Maidment – the man who could recognize his new face – and, raising his pistol, he fired. Once again Maidment was lucky. Zabel's heavy breathing had disturbed his aim, and the bullet flew harmlessly upwards. He fired again, but Maidment, his quarry in sight, was beyond caring, and did not pause.

Gunther did not hear the shots on the stairs – the sounds had not penetrated the heavily-insulated fire doors. Even those in the corridor had been no louder than the beats of a muffled drum, but nevertheless, when he had managed to pick himself up from the floor of Zabel's bedroom, draw his own pistol and peer cautiously around the door, he was surprised to see no sign of interest. Either guests in the neighbouring rooms were sleeping very soundly, or they were cowering under their bedclothes. Neither, more importantly, was there any sign of a uniform.

Quickly Gunther assessed the situation. Clearly Maidment had arrived at the hotel alone, or in advance of the authorities, and had pulled a gun on Zabel. He made up his mind, quickly retrieved his stick and hobbled to the lift. Zabel's kick had done his ankle no good at all, but he was determined to reach Geneva if he could. Zabel, he thought sourly, could take care of himself; it was Trina who needed his help.

He weighed the advantages of collecting his possessions from his room, but he had left nothing essential, and he decided against it. It was more important to get out of the hotel. But as the lift reached the ground floor and the doors opened he realized bitterly that he had left it too late. Uniformed police and plain-clothes officers were fanning out across the lobby. Arndt Gunther saw no reason to die. He quickly threw his gun down beside him. Then he dropped his stick and hobbled out of the lift, hands held high.

Twenty-three

Slowly Rory Maidment opened his eyes. As his vision grew less blurred he found he was in bed in a neat, white room with an antiseptic smell. How he came to be in a hospital he had no immediate idea. Tentatively he moved his limbs, and as he did so a nurse, who had been sitting by the window, came to his bedside.

'Ah, you're awake,' she said in French, her fingers on his pulse. 'How are you?'

'How am I?' Maidment replied a little vaguely. His shoulder was heavily bandaged, and hurt when he lifted his arm, but apart from that, and a feeling that he had just reluctantly roused from a deep sleep, there seemed to be nothing amiss.

'Can you see a friend?' the nurse asked eventually.

'There's nothing I'd like more,' said Maidment, 'and some explanations.' But memories had already begun to return – staggering down the fire stairs at the Hôtel d'Esterre, blood soaking his shirt, in mad pursuit of Horst Zabel. There had been more shooting, but at that point his mind obstinately became blank. Clearly he had been lucky, though he must have blacked out. But what about Zabel? And Mrs Carpenter? What had happened? He had to know. If they had escaped, and Derek . . .

At that point, the nurse showed in Campbell-Rose. He looked tired, but cheerful. He pulled up a chair beside the bed, and sat down on it. The nurse shut the door behind her as she left the room.

'Good morning,' he said. 'Sorry I've no grapes or flowers

or anything, but I've been busy – mostly clearing up after you. You've managed to get yourself wanted by the police forces of at least three countries – the English, the French and the Swiss – not to speak of a variety of security services, and every media man worth his salt.'

'Bloody hell!' said Maidment. 'You know as much as I do – almost.' Maidment was recovering fast, and sounded irritable. 'What happened? Did you get Zabel?'

'No.' Campbell-Rose shook his head, but when Maidment groaned aloud, he relented and added, 'You got him. A neat bit of shooting, if I may say so. I suspect it was chance, but . . . He's dead, a round straight between the eyes. You had a shoulder wound, but they got the bullet out, and I'm told it's minor. Anyway, hence your sudden notoriety. Everyone wants to know the rest of the story. None of the authorities are quite clear whether you're a villain or a hero – whether to charge you with manslaughter, at least, or give you a medal. The latter, I think.'

'I see.' Maidment was trying to get used to the idea that he had shot a man – an evil man, a dangerous man, but a man to whom he had never so much as spoken one word. He felt no compunction, but no joy.

'You acted quickly,' he said finally.

'Yes,' said Campbell-Rose. 'I had less difficulty than I expected. We've been making a few inquiries of our own, you know, and been in touch with our contacts – and your brother-in-law in London and a *juge d'instruction* in France called Grandin had made reports that tied up with your story.'

'I see,' said Maidment again. 'And what about Mrs Carpenter?'

'She was found unconscious, with a head wound and badly bruised, in the courtyard of your house in Geneva. I won't bore you with the details, but she'd managed to free herself, and probably phoned Zabel to warn him. We've got her safe, and Mr Carpenter, who says his name is Gunther. Neither of them is going to be a free citizen again for a great many years.'

Campbell-Rose paused. 'And there's another bit of good news.'

Maidment looked up sharply. 'What? Not Derek?'

'I'm afraid not. It's Peter Bingham. He's out of danger, though it'll be a long time before he's back to normal.'

'Thank God for that, at least!' Maidment passed a hand over his face to hide his feelings. 'Derek – anything at all?'

'No,' Campbell-Rose said. 'So far we've learnt nothing. The girl – Mrs Carpenter, if that's her real name – refuses to say a word. Gunther swears he doesn't know where Nana Smith kept the boy, or anything about her. But we'll find her.'

'Yes. I hope you do. Derek said she was kind, but . . .' Maidment's voice was tight. 'It may be silly, but I'd like to know exactly what happened to him.'

He was to know sooner than he – or Campbell-Rose – expected.

★

In fact, by the time they were talking, Derek Maidment had already been found. Betty Drayton and her brother Simon lived on the edge of Hampstead Heath and every morning, before they went to school, they took their dog for a walk. Betty was nine and Simon a year younger. The dog, an Alsatian, was also young, and less obedient than he might have been.

This morning he had torn his lead from Simon's grasp and made off by himself. Eventually they found him, growling at what looked like two bodies lying on the ground. Betty ran and seized the dog by his collar.

'It's – it's an old woman and a boy,' she said, blocking her brother's view. 'I think they're dead.'

'Let me see. I've never seen anyone dead.'

'No. We must go home at once and tell Mummy. She'll

know what to do.'

The children arrived home, breathless and excited. Mrs Drayton had to be persuaded to call the police, but it was only twenty minutes later that Betty and Simon were proudly leading the way for their mother and two uniformed officers.

'Along here – near the pond,' Betty said. Then, suddenly, she screamed.

A small figure in a grey flannel suit and a white shirt was staggering to his feet beside the old woman. A rug trailed on the grass behind him. Derek had awakened only moments ago and, like his father in Lausanne, couldn't imagine where he was.

'Okay. Keep the kids here.' One of the officers waved Betty and Simon back to their mother, and went forward to Derek. 'Hello, sonny,' he said gently. 'What are you doing here, eh? And who's this?'

Derek looked at him. 'It's Nana Smith,' he said. 'I can't wake her up.'

'Nanny Smith?' The policeman bent down and briefly examined the woman. It was obvious that she was dead, but he had no wish to frighten the boy. 'You'd better come along with us, young man,' he said. 'I'm afraid your nanny's not too well. She'll need an ambulance.'

Derek stared at the officer. He was trying to remember. He'd had supper and watched television and gone to sleep, though he couldn't remember going to bed. Then he'd woken here, wherever he was. Nana must have brought him during the night for some reason. Now it was morning, and he was hungry, cold, and still very sleepy. He yawned.

'Come along,' the police officer repeated. He went to pick up Derek's rug, and his eye caught sight of the brown bag under the bush. 'Is this yours?' he asked, pulling it out.

'Yes,' said Derek. Then, 'Where are you taking me?'

'To Hampstead police station, till we find out where you've come from. And what about telling us your name?'

'Hampstead?' Derek's face brightened. So that was why

the place looked vaguely familiar. He didn't recognize the spot, but he had often walked over the Heath with Uncle Geoffrey and Aunt Julia. 'That's – that's super!' he exclaimed. 'My name's Derek Maidment,' and he eagerly began to explain about the Lintons.

The police officers exchanged glances, as they remembered the names the sergeant had read out to them at their routine briefing the previous day. 'So you're Derek Maidment,' the one who had been doing all the talking said, 'and Geoffrey Linton's your uncle, you say? Well, we'll have to see, won't we? Get in touch with him, we will.'

'Yes,' said Derek. 'Please!' He took one look at the body of Nana Smith, then allowed himself to be led away.

*

Geoffrey Linton was on the point of leaving for the office when the police phoned. He was late, but when he heard the news he forgot his impatience. He ran up the stairs two at a time and burst into the bedroom where Julia was dressing.

'I'm going to fetch him now. You'd better call Rory and tell him we've got Derek. And you can tell him we're damn well keeping the boy till we know exactly what's been going on. I told you how cagey the security boys were being.'

'Yes! Yes!' At that moment Julia would have agreed to anything.

She hurriedly finished dressing, inspected Derek's room and turned on his electric blanket. Then she phoned her brother, first at his house, then when there was no answer, at the Consulate.

Finally a voice she didn't recognize said, 'Mrs Linton, this is Hugh Cantley. I had you put through to me because we've met. Do you remember? At a dinner given by the Grants.'

'Of course, Mr Cantley. But Rory –'

'He's not here, Mrs Linton. He's in Lausanne, and I'm afraid he's in hospital. He's had an – an accident, I gather.

Nothing serious. The bullet's been extracted.'

'What did you say – bullet?'

'I'm sorry, yes, but I assure you he's in no danger and he's something of a hero, though why I've no idea.' Cantley let his irritation show. After all, Rory Maidment was his deputy and surely Campbell-Rose could have been more explicit. 'If it's urgent I'll try to get a message through to him. That's the best I can do, I'm afraid.'

'It *is* urgent – very urgent.' Julia thought quickly; she could hear Geoffrey's car returning, and she must be at the door to greet Derek. 'Tell him to call me as soon as possible, please. Tell him that Derek, his son, is safe with us.'

In the event it was Campbell-Rose who called back. He spoke to Linton and permitted himself to explain something of the situation. By then Derek, having had a large breakfast and a hot bath, was once more asleep, tucked up by Julia in his own bed. Maidment was also asleep, but Campbell-Rose didn't hesitate to wake him.

'And he's all right?'

'Fine. He's been well fed and well cared for and, needless to say, he wants to see you.'

'When?'

'That depends on the doctor. And on the people waiting to question you – and Derek – but either the Lintons will bring him out here, or you can go back to the UK. You'll be due sick leave anyway, I guess. Meanwhile I'll see you get a phone.'

'Thanks.'

Maidment blinked away tears of joy and exhaustion as Campbell-Rose left him. Derek was alive and safe. It didn't matter how or why. God, he was grateful! There was so much to be grateful for. His vistas – his options – were opening again. Derek and, if she would have him, Marie-Louise. When the phone came, it was Marie-Louise he called first.

X